THE OBSERVER
IN THE ROYAL NAVY
1908–2003

THE OBSERVER

IN THE ROYAL NAVY

1908–2003

AN ILLUSTRATED HISTORY
BY K M DAVIES

SERENDIPITY

Copyright © K M Davies 2005

First published in 2005 by
Serendipity
First Floor
37/39 Victoria Road
Darlington
DL1 5SF

British Library Catalogue-in-Publication data
A catalogue record for this book is available from the British Library

ISBN 1 84394 154 6

Designed by Don Friston

Printed and bound by CPI Antony Rowe, Eastbourne

Cover illustrations:
Fowsey biplane (*modified Maurice Farman*)
Sea King helicopter AEW 2

INTRODUCTION

Many publications are available covering the history of the Fleet Air Arm. They describe the development of naval aircraft and their operation from aircraft carriers, from the early days as a potential asset to the efficiency of the Royal Navy, to the present time, when they play an essential part in naval operations.

The pilots have already received the acclamation which is their due; in this monograph I endeavour to trace the development of the art and craft of the airborne observer in the Royal Navy, from the original conception of their duties to the present day. During this period of 95 years, they have been asked to train for and perform an increasing number of different tasks. Today they operate in a world of high technology and make a huge contribution to naval and combined operations.

My own experience, as an observer, from 1951 to 1959 in 814 NAS (A/S Firefly 6s and Avengers), 825 NAS (A/S Gannets) and 849 NAS (AEW Skyraiders) has given me an enduring pleasure in the company of, and respect for, all naval aviators. Long may they fly!

Keith Davies

ACKNOWLEDGEMENTS

I am greatly indebted for the assistance received from the staff of the National Archives, The Fleet Air Arm Museum, and also the Fleet Air Arm Officers' Association.

Individuals who deserve special and sincere thanks are: Ray Sturtivant for allowing me to make use of his encyclopaedic knowledge of naval aircraft; Dr Jane Harold, Archivist at Britannia Royal Naval College, for post-1960 initial observer training; and Douglas Bartlett, for the use of his father's diaries and flying logbook.

Past and present members of the FAAOA have helped with information from their individual service experiences. Lt Cdr M C S Apps RN, Korea; Cdr D W Besley RN, ASW training, sonobuoys; Lt Cdr R D McCulloch RN, Sea Venom CCAs; Lt Cdr A G H Perkins RN, observer/pilot conversion; Cdr A G B Philip RN, observer training, AEW; Lt Cdr P J Wilkins RN, all-weather fighters; also Lt Cdr J Waterman RD RNR, for his good wishes and encouragement as editor of *Fly Navy* and author of *The Fleet Air Arm History*.

I have made efforts to acknowledge all copyright holders; anyone who has been inadvertantly left out should contact me, and I will arrange for an acknowledgement should the monograph be reprinted.

In conclusion, I must also thank my friend, Don Friston, for his expertise in the editing and presentation of the final product. I hope the content is worthy of the encouragement he has contributed.

CONTENTS

LIST OF ILLUSTRATIONS

FROM 1908 TO THE END
OF WORLD WAR I

THE NAVY'S EARLY INTEREST IN FLYING

The Admiralty's first firm interest in aircraft for naval reconnaissance was in 1908, and in 1911 the duties required from an observer specialist were listed as follows:

1 Ascertain what vessels were in enemy ports, if they were invisible from a blockading squadron.

2 Ascend from a floating base and ascertain if any enemy squadron was in the vicinity.

3 Fly above the fleet and locate submarines.

4 Detect minefields.

5 Direct the fire of the guns of the fleet.

The Committee of Imperial Defence considered the future of aerial navigation for naval and military purposes and, in 1912, the Royal Flying Corps was established with naval and military wings.

In 1913, for the first time, aircraft played a part in naval manoeuvres in the North Sea. They made submarine and surface ship sightings, and communicated successfully by wireless telegraphy to the ships. Training was haphazard, and use was made of naval and army officers for specialist tasks e.g. spotting for guns, and ship identification. Young, lightly-built mid-shipmen were often used to save weight in underpowered aircraft. In July 1914 the Naval Wing became the Royal Naval Air Service.

WORLD WAR I

In 1914, as the war developed, so did the tasks undertaken by the RNAS: anti-submarine patrols by seaplanes in the North Sea; long distance bombing attacks into enemy territory, notably on the Friedrichshafen Zeppelin sheds by Avro 504s, severely damaging one Zeppelin and destroying a gas manu-facturing plant. Reconnaissance and aerial spotting for artillery was carried out for the army.

The Gallipoli campaign, in 1915, showed the potential of naval air power with the RNAS operating from seaplane tenders and the island of Tenedos.

The flight line at Tenedos. Cdr Samson's BE2a No. 50 in foreground

Commander Samson describes the many and varied operations carried out by his wing in his book *Fights and Flights*. "We were busily engaged in mine spotting and spotting for battleships engaging shore batteries. A Farman, spotting for HMS *Agamemnon*, reported that they had completely destroyed three out of four howitzers in a battery that had been firing on the fleet and landing place. I made it a rule for each aeroplane as far as possible to carry bombs, and to drop them when a good target was seen." Turkish supplies were landed by sea on the peninsula and these bases made ideal bombing targets. The Germans commented "Terrible was the effect of these missiles on the transport columns and disembarkation points." In addition, constant anti-submarine and frequent anti-aircraft patrols were carried out. The army, as a result of reconnaissance flights, was supplied with maps of enemy positions made from mosaics of low-level photographs.

In 1915, a notable achievement in another area of conflict was the destruction of the German cruiser *Konigsberg*. She was taking refuge in the Rufigi River in German East Africa and was hit by naval gunfire directed from the air by observer S/Lt Arnold. Two aircraft were used for spotting between 6 and 11 July, one observer flying a total of nine hours in one day.

Also during 1915, HMS *Campania* was commissioned and successfully flew seaplanes, fitted with wheels, from her flight deck. Oliver Schwann, her CO, commented in his report on her 6 months trials "The Observers (RNR Midshipmen) had to be taught signalling, observation work, and the meaning of initiative,"

Meanwhile, the RNAS was concentrating hard on the anti-submarine war in the North Sea. Seaplane patrols were augmented by attacks on submarine bases by the Dunkirk Wing with attacks on Zeebrugge and Antwerp. Non-rigid airships and kite balloons also played their part. Admiral Sir John Fisher, the First Sea Lord, initiated the use of airships against submarines. The SS1

(Submarine Scout) employed the envelope of a small rigid airship with the fuselage of a BE2 suspended below.

By the end of 1915 there were nine SS airships in commission, stationed on both sides of the Channel, in Wales and in Northern Ireland. Although not sinking any U-boats, they effectively kept them down. Kite balloons tethered to ships at sea increased the area under observation, with the observer connected to the ship by telephone.

Observation balloon operating off Gallipoli 1915. The observer is about to board the basket at the nearest corner to the photographer

In 1915, there was a small group of commissioned observers, who were supplemented by RNVR officers, but by March 1916 the total number of observers was seventy-eight.

In 1916, a seaplane launched from HMS *Engadine* sighted units of the German High Seas Fleet. Reports were received in the W/T office of *Engadine*, and retransmitted, but were not received by Admiral Beatty. This vital intelligence might well have helped to give a more decisive outcome to the Battle of Jutland.

THE OBSERVER OFFICER

In 1916 the rank of Observer Officer was created and, in 1917, the integration of aircraft into the general work of the fleet led to a more structured approach to observer training. In 1917, the first organised course was started at Eastchurch. The course included seamanship, W/T navigation, intelligence, bomb dropping, and aerial gunnery. Observer's wings were introduced.

The following are extracts from the diary and log of Stanley Bartlett, who joined the RNAS in 1915 as a wireless operator and later became a commissioned observer. In addition to searching sea and sky, he was at different times, wireless operator, bomb aimer, and air gunner. His pilot was responsible for the navigation of the aircraft until Bartlett qualified as an observer. He was demobilised from the RAF in February 1919.

DIARY AND FLYING LOG

1915

1 Nov – Today I joined the RNAS at Brook Green, Hammersmith, London.

2 Nov – Arrived at Talbot Motor Works the training establishment for wireless operators in Chiswick at 8 a.m. I was told the course would be: wireless lectures, practical work, buzzer, flashing, semaphore, naval flags, map reading, and naval procedure. The routine was as follows:

0830 Fall in for inspection; 0900–1000 Buzzer on circuit; 1100–1230 Route march; 1230–1400 Lunch; 1400 Roll call then practical work – W/T sets, relays etc.; 1530–1615 naval routines; 1615–1700 W/T procedures; 1700–1800 flashing.

1916

By the middle of February my tickets were appearing on the board and any day I expected to be transferred, and on the 28th I was informed that my posting was to Killingholme on the river Humber.

29 Feb – Went down to White City, London, to collect £1,500 worth of wireless gear, then by train to Grimsby. 2100 arrived at Killingholme Air Station, one of the largest seaplane bases in England.

31 March – Received first signals from a seaplane.

7 April – Paddle Fleet Messenger HMS *Killingholme* damaged North Sea. Received W/T transmission, decoded and reported it to CO.

25 April – 0330 called out to fit W/T in 225 hp Short seaplane.

27 April – HMS *Killinghome* torpedoed.

2 July – First flight in a 225 hp Short 184 seaplane. Flew about 35 miles in 40 minutes at 1,000 ft. It was rather bumpy and I was not very impressed with flying after this trip.

24 July – My second flight 50 miles in 65 minutes up to 2,500 ft, calm day, and good W/T communication with base.

1 Aug – My third flight. First bombing exercise. W/T results good.

14 Aug – Rifle and machine gun practice on range.

26 Aug – Practice spotting exercise. Verey light target position, smoke bomb fall of shot. I had to report by W/T distance bombs were from target. Comment by Wing Commander "Very good observing."

28 Sept – Revolver practice and bomb dropping sights explained.

1 Oct – Flight to communicate with submarine on W/T, very good result.

4 Oct – Send to sub on flashing lamp and semaphore.

9 Oct – Bomb submarine.

13 Oct – Bombing sub with dummy bombs. Go on board sub to work W/T as several vain trips had been attempted to communicate with her. Good contact was established and maintained with seaplane. Both operators commended by CO.

23 Oct – Flight to observe submarine at torpedo practice. Good W/T results communicating with ground station and Short seaplane. During my watch from 2130 to midnight, I was told that two W/T machines were to be away at dawn and I was to go in one. I was preparing the aircraft until 0145 the following morning.

24 Oct – Called at 0430 took off at 0630 to look for German fleet. For two hours in good W/T communication with base, then pilot came down so low my aerial touched the water and carried away. A little later the pilot decided to land on the sea, but looking below was surprised to see fields and villages. After flying east for 10 miles, saw what was thought to be water, but it was thick mist about 20 feet above the water. We pancaked from this height, and found the port float badly smashed and two main struts badly bent. The pilot steered for land and after 45 minutes tried to run ashore but got stuck in the mud and had to wait for the tide to come in to take the plane to the beach. The handling party arrived in the afternoon and we arrived at the air station at 2030 after the longest, and hardest, day's work in my life.

Paddle Fleet Messenger, able to service seaplanes and based at Immingham

FLYING LOG 1916 – Jul to Oct

Flight	Date	Pilot	A/C	Hrs min	Remarks
1	2 July	LT Iron	Short 184	45	W/T
2	24 July	FSL Arundel		1 10	W/T
3	1 Aug	FSL Morse		50	W/T
4	8 Aug	FSL Simpson		1 05	W/T and bombs
5	22 Aug	SL Arundel		45	W/T
6	26 Aug	LT Hards DSC		45	Spotting
7	11 Sept	FSL Smith		1 10	W/T
8	18 Sept	FSL Arundel		50	Keeping station
9	21 Sept	FSL Arundel		1 00	W/T submarine
10	26 Sept	FSL Arundel		1 15	Patrol
11	2 Oct	LT Hards DSC		35	Bomb dropping
12	12 Oct	FSL Dubuc		35	Bomb dropping
13	13 Oct	FSL Popham		40	Bomb dropping
14	16 Oct	FSL Arundel		30	Bomb dropping
15	16 Oct	FSL Arundel		40	Bomb dropping
16	17 Oct	FSL Hughes		45	Bomb dropping
17	21 Oct	FSL Corey-Wright		1 30	W/T submarine
18	22 Oct	FSL Wilkes		45	Bomb dropping
19	23 Oct	FSL Wilkes		1 30	Bomb dropping
20	24 Oct	FSL Wilkes		2 30	Patrol

Short 184, bombed up

1917

23 Jan – Flight firing explosive bullets at balloon sent up from the ground. Fired 12 shots from Lewis gun. Engine packed up, towed home by ML.

15 Feb – Patrol war channel to Cromer and back. Fine trip, obtaining excellent W/T results, being in perfect communication with base and receiving at the maximum distance of 65 miles. Later the CO sent for a copy of the log.

16 Feb – A patrol to Scarborough at 1600, engine trouble near Flamborough Head, land in sea, and taxi for one and a half hours, then beach machine at Kilnsea battery, working on till 2300 to anchor the machine. A rotten job having to wade out into the sea and dig the anchors into the sand.

3 May – Patrol war channel to Flamborough Head. We escort cargo boats and pass over destroyers and MLs. In the air for two hours and fifty minutes.

8 May – Ordered to proceed to Eastchurch for Bombing and Gunnery Course.

14 May – Arrived Eastchurch. A very nice but strict station.

18 May – Getting on very well but a frightful lot to learn.

23 May – On aerial rifle range firing at planes crossing on wires; obtained three hits.

28 May – Pass out on bombs and sights.

29 May – Two flights over mirror, and bomb dropping.

The Mirror – Two bomb sights were in use: The Reverse Lens Bomb Sight and the Central Flying School Bomb Sight with Periscope.

30 May – Leysdown – ground machine gun firing. I do well. Flight firing Lewis gun from Morris Shorthorn, good results.

4 June – Exam results: Bombs V.G.   Frames V.G.   Sights V.G.   Machine Gun V.G.   Summary V.G.

6 June – Leave Eastchurch 0730, arrive Killingholme 2100.

FLYING LOG 1917 – Jan to May

Flight	Date	Pilot	A/C	Hrs min	Remarks
21	2 Jan	FSL Pearce	Short 184	1 00	W/T
22	23 Jan	FSL Popham		45	Lewis gun at balloons
23	8 Feb	FSL Arundel		1 25	Patrol
24	12 Feb	FSL Arundel		30	Patrol
25	15 Feb	FSL Pearce		3 15	Patrol
26	16 Feb	FSL Popham		45	Patrol
27	3 May	FSL Ellis		2 50	Patrol
28	28 May	LT Wallace		10	Weapons course Eastchurch
					Bomb dropping
29	28 May	LT Wallace		20	Bomb dropping
30	29 May	LT Bowater		20	Bomb dropping
31	30 May	LT Arnold DSO		20	Aerial gunnery

27 June – Called 0445, off water in H12 at 0450. Very misty, patrol to Whitby. On return journey enemy submarine sighted [and] 100 lb bomb dropped, sub submerged, no further sighting. I obtain our position from Flamborough W/T station and inform base that we have bombed enemy submarine in position indicated. Return 0940 after a fine trip, the W/T worked very well.

6 July – 1400 trip in H12, patrol to Flamborough, then in an easterly direction. When about 30 miles east of Spurn, starboard engine packs up, plane side slips and pilot stops port engine and makes a fine landing on the water. We start port engine and taxi homewards; had to stand on the extreme edge of the port wing to keep the machine balanced. At 1830 we sighted a patrol vessel, which put us on course to Spurn. Arrived at base at 2315, absolutely drenched.

23 Aug – Called 0530 for H12 patrol to look for hostile aircraft, but no luck. After flying for three and a half hours, we sighted a German destroyer, which

fired several rounds at us. Having no bombs we broke away and resumed our patrol, returning to base at 1400. This was longest trip I have ever had, being up for seven hours.

3 Sept – Patrol in H12 with a Short and a Schneider, following an enemy torpedo attack on a coastal convoy, saw a damaged vessel under tow.

17 Sept – Patrol in a Short south to Spurn; when about 20 miles southeast see bubbles and foam from apparent hostile submarine. Drop two 100lb bombs, no further sighting.

15 Oct – Reported to CO at Observer School, Eastchurch. Local flight pm. Then medical, followed by stiff educational test the next day. Left at 1530 for Killingholme.

Curtiss H12
Large America

FLYING LOG 1917 – Jun to Nov

Flight	Date	Pilot	A/C	Hrs min	Remarks
32	27 June	FC Hards	H12	4 00	Bombed German sub.
33	6 July	LT Robertson	H12	3 00	Patrol forced landing
34	16 July	FC Hards	H12	3 00	Patrol
35	19 Aug	FC Travers	H12	4 00	Patrol Scarborough

continued

Flying Log 1917 – Jun to Nov, *continued*

Flight	Date	Pilot	A/C	Hrs min	Remarks
36	20 Aug	LT Scott	H12	3 00	Patrol Cromer
37	22 Aug	FC Hards	H12	7 00	Patrol off Holland. Fired at by German destroyer
38	3 Sept	FC Hards	H12	3 00	Patrol
39	6 Sept	FC Travers	H12	30	Patrol
40	10 Sept	FC Travers	H12	3 00	Patrol
41	17 Sept	FC Travers	Short 184	2 30	Two bombs dropped on unidentified object – submarine?
42	16 Oct	LT Everett	BE	20	Test trip Eastchurch
43	1 Nov	FC Travers	Nieuport	20	Aerial gunnery

1 Nov – Commission papers through. Flight in a Nieuport, firing at balloons.

3 Nov – Report to Crystal Palace and receive discharge papers. Visiting Admiralty, the following days and buying a new uniform.

10 Nov – Eastchurch – started instruction, three months course – (see opposite).

On 2 Dec 1917, there were 127 trainee observers at Eastchurch. Three were Observer Lieutenants, five Observer Sub Lieutenants, and 119 Probationary Observer Officers. Some of the latter were W/T and gunnery ratings who were commissioned, having proved their worth in the air, and others were direct officer entry into the RNAS.

Short 184 (225) with the observer holding a large camera. Over 650 of these aircraft were issued to the RNAS and used for searches and bombing. (225 = engine hp)

COPY OF PAGE FROM FLYING LOGBOOK

Date and Hour.	Direction and Velocity	Machine Type and No.	Passenger / Pilot	Time in Air	Height	Course	Remarks

FLYING LOG – Nov 1917 to Mar 1918

Flight	Date	Pilot	A/C	Hrs min	Remarks
44	11 Nov	FL Stevenson	BE	25	First flight as Commissioned Observer over Sheerness
45	11 Nov	FL Fowler	BE	20	Looped three times
46	12 Nov	FL Stevenson	BE	25	Sketch Sheppey Island
47	10 Dec	LT Chapman	Fowsey	25	Bomb dropping
48	10 Dec	WO Grady	Fowsey	40	Bomb dropping
49	10 Dec	WO Grady	Fowsey	1 35	Bomb dropping
50	15 Dec	LT Roach	Fowsey	30	Bomb dropping
51	18 Dec	WO Grady	Be	10	Bomb dropping
52	18 Dec	WO Grady	Be	5	Dud engine
53	19 Dec	LT Bowater	Fowsey	45	Bomb dropping
54	19 Dec	LT Bowater	Fowsey	35	Bomb dropping
1918…					
55	7 Jan	FSL Stevenson	BE 8426	40	Reconnaissance
56	10 Jan	FSL Everett	Nieuport 9238	25	Reconnaissance
57	10 Jan	FSL Shepherd	BE 957	20	Rec
58	14 Jan	LT Lawson	Nieuport	15	Rec
59	14 Jan	LT Roberts	Fowsey 6312	13	Rec
60	14 Jan	LT Roberts	Fowsey	17	Visual circuits
61	5 Feb	FSL Everett	BE	40	Rec Leysdown
62	13 Feb	FS Thompson	BE	23	Rec
63	18 Feb	LT Lawson	BE	1 00	Rec
64	18 Feb	LT Mcgregor	BE	14	Rec
65	18 Feb	LT Mcgregor	BE	31	Rec
66	23Feb	FSL Thompson	BE	28	W/T
67	23 Feb	FSL Alexander	BE	20	W/T
68	23 Feb	FSL Alexander	BE	17	W/T
69	25 Feb	FSL Fowler	BE	14	Gunnery
70	25 Feb	FSL Richards	BE	33	Rec
71	25 Feb	FSL Thompson	BE	37	Rec
72	25 Feb	FSL Thompson	DH4	1 00	Photo 14000 ft

continued

Flying Log – Nov 1917 to Mar 1918, *continued*

Flight	Date	Pilot	A/C	Hrs min	Remarks
73	27 Feb	FSL Everett	BE	14	Rec
74	13 March	FSL Emery	Fowsey	11	Lewis gun
75	13 March	FSL Wallis	Fowsey	5	Lewis gun
76	13 March	FSL Emery	Fowsey	17	Lewis gun
77	14 March	FSL Wallis	Fowsey	11	Lewis gun
78	15 March	FSL Emery	Fowsey	6	Lewis gun
79	15 March	FSL Wallis	Fowsey	11	Lewis gun

FSL = Flight Sub Lieutenant

The Fowsey aircraft mentioned in the logbook (see page 11) is a modified Maurice Farman. These became known as the Eastchurch type, or Fowsey (N 6310 is pictured here). N 6312 was modified on 14.8.17 by replacing the 80 hp Renault engine with one of 170 hp.

Diary continued:

10 March – Started exams, result was very favourable to myself. I asked to be sent to a seaplane station. Sent on home leave pending appointment.

20 March – Appointed to Dundee, reported there on the 22nd.

26 March – First patrol with Ensign Foster USN who landed 10 miles NE of Aberdeen and beached the machine.

27 March – Towed into Peterhead harbour, machine considered being in too bad a state to fly back.

28 April – Patrol with Ensign Keyes, USN. After 5 hours engine conked and we landed in a terribly rough sea 4 miles from land. The waves were 15 ft high and the plane was breaking up. We were spotted by an airship and asked them to inform Dundee and send immediate assistance. After two hours a merchant ship picked us up and put into Arbroath with the dismantled machine and us. We returned to Dundee two days later.

May–Oct – During this period, flying patrols and convoy protection in Shorts, our observer suffered five engine failures.

11 Nov – Armistice Day. The greatest excitement and joy one has ever experienced, everyone went mad.

11 December – Last flight, before Rt. Hon. Winston Churchill, MP for Dundee. Total flying time in RNAS 302 hours 34 minutes

At this time there were 306 Observers on the Navy List.

Gt Yarmouth Naval Air Station

THE OVERALL PICTURE

In 1917, the U-boat campaign was at its height. Coastal submarines, some laying mines, would transit on the surface near to the North Hinder light vessel to conserve battery power. Previous attempts to use flying boats in the A/S role proved unsuccessful, as they could not cope with sea conditions on the East coast. Then Lt J C Porte, later Wing Commander, succeeded in modifying Curtiss Americas to combat the increasing threat in the North Sea. More powerful engines, redesigned hulls and planing bottoms gave greater stability, and better take off and landing performance in the

*The Farman
Longhorn was
the first aircraft
to land at Great
Yarmouth, in
May 1913*

*F2A flying-boat.
Note the port
gun hatch,
semaphore
signal arms and
screened pilot's
cockpit (the
previous models
had no screens).
Seven machine
guns provided
defence. In May
1918, four F2As
shot down six
out of fourteen
attacking planes*

H12 (Large America) and the later Felixstowe F2A. Operating from RNAS stations at Felixstowe, Great Yarmouth, and Killingholme, these flying boats were tasked to carry out reconnaissance over the North Sea and to attack U-boats and Zeppelins.

A plan, called the Spiders Web, helped pilots to patrol the North Sea. Using the North Hinder light vessel as a central base point, an octagonal figure was drawn with eight arms radiating 30 miles from the base. Lines linked the arms at 10, 20, and 30 miles from the base. The three sections in each sector would be surveyed twice on any patrol, and two sectors (one quarter of the web) overflown in less than five hours. The endurance of the aircraft was six hours at 60 knots.

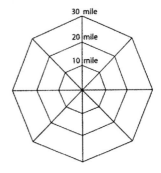

Extract from H12 logs 1917:

14 May – Zeppelin L22 shot down
20 May – UC36 sunk
14 June – Zeppelin L43 shot down
28 Sept – UC6 bombed

The new Inshore Anti-Submarine Observers School was formed at Aldeburgh in August 1918. The airfield was a land plane satellite of Great Yarmouth. This was merged with the No.1 Marine Naval Air Service Observers School at the end of the year, under the control of the RAF, with which the RNAS had amalgamated in April 1918. At this time the Royal Navy had one flush deck carrier and 126 naval air stations.

BETWEEN THE WARS 1918–1939

A period of intense bickering went on between the two sections of the RAF for the first three years. Almost all the naval officers, when experienced in air operations, drifted away from the Royal Navy to the RAF. Frequently, men with no naval training were detailed for service at sea. Air Naval Gunnery Observers flew for gunfire spotting, but all searches were by RAF observers.

An initial step to remedy the situation was taken in 1919. The RAF realised a separate wing had to be established to train aircrew for the specialised flying required by the Royal Navy. The Fleet Air Arm of the RAF was formed at Gosport, which became known as RAF Gosport Fleet Air Arm Station. In 1920 an Observer Training Fight was formed there.

After discussions in the Inter Services Committee it was agreed, in 1921, that RN observers should be trained at the School of Naval Co-operation at Lee-on-Solent. Courses were held at six monthly intervals. After the first two courses, they consisted of two weeks gunnery at Whale Island, six weeks at the Signal School, Eastleigh, five months training at Lee, then six months probationary service at Gosport. Training aircraft included the Fairey IIIF, the Avro Bison, the Blackburn Ripon, Baffin, and Shark; and after 1937, the Fairey Swordfish.

Fairey IIIF. This three-seat strike aircraft became the most widely used inter-war type in the FAA, entering service in 1928. However, it was not fitted with an arrester hook, and was declared obsolete in 1940

Another compromise was reached in 1924, when it was agreed that the Fleet Air Arm of the RAF was to include shipboard aircraft only. All observers were to be appointed by the Royal Navy to the parent ships and lent to the RAF (Fleet Air Arm) squadrons. They performed watch-keeping and divisional duties in these ships. The main share of advancing aviation knowledge in the Fleet fell to the observers. 70% of pilots were to be RN but held two commissions, RN and RAF.

The Avro Bison started service at Gosport in 1923. It incorporated a large cabin for the needs of the observer and radio operator, including a chart table and wireless apparatus. It was withdrawn from service in 1929

The aircraft used were in the proportion of one fighter aircraft to two reconnaissance, the latter performing all the strike and scouting roles, as well as spotting for ships gunfire. The observers were mainly employed in the TSR roles, but also as navigation leaders and W/T operators in two-seat fighters; also in seaplanes and amphibians in battleships and cruisers. They were required to report the position of enemy ships up to 150 miles away to within

Blackburn Shark. This three-seat TBR started service in 1931, becoming second line after 1938

a four-mile circle of accuracy; shadowing and reporting the course to within 10% and speed within two knots; also identifying ships by class and name. After four hours, they would navigate back to within visual range of the ship.

Essential to accurate navigation was to be aware of changes in the direction and speed of the wind, and the following method of wind finding was used: Observer to pilot, "Stand by to find a wind – Stand by to drop, drop." Observer starts stopwatch to time smoke float hitting the sea (taken from a table showing time taken to fall from different release heights) and, when the s/f hit the sea, tells the pilot: "Stand by to turn, turn." Pilot starts a rate two turn – a 180-degree turn in 90 seconds. After 90 seconds on course, turn a/c on to original course, again a rate two turn. After 90 seconds on this course, bearing taken on s/f. This gives a reciprocal of the wind direction. Times are then taken when the s/f is on the beam, and the quarter, to fix the distance from the s/f, and to calculate the wind speed from the 6 minutes of drift.

Fairey Swordfish II. This type entered service in 1936 and flew throughout the war

A Naval Air Expansion Programme was started in 1934 and approval was given "To instruct officers for observer training if insufficient volunteers were forthcoming." This was used intermittently until 1936. In 1937 the RN took full responsibility for FAA and, in 1938, the first Short Commission scheme was introduced. Observers and pilots entered for air duties and had limited executive powers. They became known as the Air Branch of the Royal Navy, with an A in the curl of their braid. Volunteer naval officers were still accepted.

To meet the need for expansion, the School of Naval Co-operation moved from Lee to Ford and became the Number One Observer School. The rules of naval command were now being applied to squadrons, so that observers could command aircraft and squadrons. Therefore, at the outbreak of war, in

1939, there was a rapidly expanding observer branch with senior officers who had been observers and understood the role and potential of air-power at sea.

In 1939 the Number Two Observer School was opened at Lee-on-Solent. Its purpose was to train a short term reserve of RNVR observer officers (in their late teens and early twenties) who had entered for one and a half years service on the active list, until the first short service officers became available. Four weeks initial training at Lee was followed by two months at St Vincent, the training establishment at Gosport. They emerged as Leading Naval Airmen, having completed a course in boatwork; signalling; ship routines; the history of the RN; knots and splices; ship and aircraft recognition; elementary navigation; and square-bashing. Then to Whale Island for a gunnery course, followed by two months of signalling and W/T at HMS Raven (Eastleigh). Practical navigation, reconnaissance techniques, meteorology, photography, and radar were taught at HMS Condor (Arbroath) and after 1940 at Piarco (Trinidad). A little polish and an introduction to officer-like qualities were provided at the Royal Naval College, Greenwich, the finishing process before they joined a squadron.

WORLD WAR II

13 December, 1939 saw the first spotting operation of the war by a Fleet Air Arm aircraft. *Graf Spee,* the German pocket battleship, met the British cruisers *Exeter, Ajax,* and *Achilles* and opened fire, damaging the two Walrus aircraft of *Exeter. Ajax* launched her Seafox, piloted by Lt Lewin RN with Lt Kearney RN as observer, who spotted for the cruisers then engaging the enemy. *Exeter* was forced to disengage to repair damage she had suffered and the Seafox closed to assess damage on *Graf Spee,* counting some 30 shell hits, before retiring to continue reporting fall of shot. Shortly afterwards the action was broken off. The Seafox was ordered to report *Exeter's* position course and speed, and was then recovered.

Graf Spee took refuge in Montevideo. The Seafox carried out daily spotting flights, and reported the *Graf Spee* had been scuttled at 2045 on 17 December.

Supermarine Walrus. Designed in 1939 as a spotter aircraft to be catapulted from cruisers, these became heavily involved in air-sea rescue duties. The last aircraft left service in 1946

Fairey Seafox. Built in 1936 as a two-seat reconnaissance seaplane, it was capable of being catapulted from a light cruiser. These aircraft were last used in 1943

NORWAY 1940

Norway provided the FAA with its first real campaign test. 800 and 804 Skua squadrons were based at Hatson, in the Orkneys, to carry out operations in the south of Norway. The German cruiser *Konigsberg* had been badly damaged by Norwegian shore batteries, at Bergen, and was reported to be lying immobilised alongside the jetty. At 0515 on 10 April 1940, the two squadrons (total 16 Skuas) took off for the 300-mile flight to Bergen, navigated by the senior observer Lt Cdr Hare RN. The Skuas pressed home their attack in 60° dives and within 10 minutes *Konigsberg* was a blazing wreck, blew up, and sank. This was the first major warship to be sunk by air attack, an historic moment.

Only three days later, while HMS *Warspite* was steaming up Ofat Fjord, her Swordfish, fitted with floats, and navigated by observer Lt Cdr W Brown, sighted and successfully attacked *U64* which was at anchor. The first U-boat to be sunk by a FAA aircraft since the start of the war.

Blackburn Skua – two-seat fighter dive-bomber

TARANTO

HMS *Illustrious* had joined the Mediterranean Fleet on 1 September 1940, becoming the platform from which the most famous of all the FAA actions was to be launched. The strike plan, to cripple the Italian Fleet, had been conceived as early as 1935, when the Italians invaded Abyssinia. The modified plan to attack Taranto envisaged a night attack, with torpedo attacks on the battleships and cruisers in the Mar Grande, plus dive-bomber strikes on ships in the Mar Picolo and the seaplane base. These were to be lit by flare droppers which would also attack the storage facilities.

By October 1940, the aircrews of 815 and 819 squadrons were well experienced in night flying. On 11 November, *Illustrious* and her escorts detached from the fleet and, at 2057, the first 12 Swordfish took off on the 170-mile flight to the target. At 2115 the formation became separated in cloud, but seven aircraft, with the leader Lt Cdr Williamson and his observer Lt Scarlett, pressed on, the remainder following independently. The second strike of Swordfish took off at 2123, led by Lt Cdr Hale and his observer Lt Carline. All aircraft reached the target and in 23 minutes the attack was completed.

Events on the night of 11–12 November showed that the FAA was the RN's most devastating weapon. In a total of six and a half hours flying time, 20 aircraft had inflicted more damage on the Italian Fleet than the German High Seas Fleet had suffered at the Battle of Jutland. Three battleships were put out of action, and a heavy cruiser and destroyers, together with the seaplane base and oil storage tanks, damaged.

HMS ARK ROYAL

At the end of the Norwegian campaign, in June 1940, '*Ark*' joined Force H based at Gibraltar. Her Swordfish, Skuas, and later Fairey Fulmars, carried out A/S patrols; searches for surface vessels; strikes for fleet and convoy protection; and also were navigation leaders for the fighter reinforcement of Malta.

Gerard Woods in *Wings At Sea* describes the observer's task in a Swordfish cockpit. "In this very confined space he has to navigate, using a Bigsworth chart board and instruments; look for surface and airborne targets; keep a listening watch on one or two radio wavelengths; be prepared to issue an enemy report which may involve using his coding machine; remember to reel his aerial out and in; use the homing beacon, and chat with the pilot to keep him awake for six hours."

In order to communicate with the fleet he would have learnt the whole of the fleet signal book, also how to send and receive 22 words per minute on the W/T buzzer, and 15 wpm by semaphore or by Aldis lamp.

Fairey Fulmar two-seat fighter/reconnaissance, 1940–1943. It was replaced by the Firefly

A further task was added in April 1941 when some Swordfish were fitted with Air Surface Vessel radar. It was said to have a range of 10 miles at 1,000ft and 30 miles at 3,000ft. The picture presented was a base line with echoes showing a bearing and distance. An early version of ASV radar was trialled in a Swordfish at Lee-on-Solent and St Athan from December 1939. The antennae were mounted on the wing struts.

Typical preparations for fighter flights from 'Ark' to Malta were briefings by observers, who prepared charts for RAF pilots with details of courses and recognition signals, plus silhouettes of any ships or aircraft they were likely to meet. Very necessary precautions to complete a 400-mile flight if a single-seat fighter became detached from the navigation leaders in Skuas and Fulmars.

BISMARCK

Meanwhile, on 21 May 1941, *Bismarck* and *Prinz Eugen* were spotted by the RAF, sailing for Bergen in Norway. In appalling weather a target-towing Maryland was manned by volunteers. The pilot, Lt Goddard RN, with Cdr G Rotdean RN, as observer, flew a reconnaissance mission the next day. Their negative report from Bergen and adjacent fjords resulted in the Home Fleet C-in-C, Sir John Tovey, putting to sea with a force which included the only available carrier, *Victorious,* with nine Swordfish of 815, and six Fulmars of 800Z squadrons on board. Force H proceeded with all despatch from Gibraltar on 24 May to intercept *Bismarck.*

During the afternoon of 24 May, *Victorious* was detached from the main force with an escort of four cruisers to mount a strike on *Bismarck.* At 2200 the strike force of nine Swordfish was despatched, followed, an hour later, by Fulmars which took on the shadowing role. A Swordfish made ASV contact at 2327 at 16 miles, 120 miles from the carrier. *Bismarck* was then sighted through the clouds. The attack was carried out through clouds and heavy gunfire, with one torpedo hit being observed.

Although the hit was on the heavy armour belt *Bismarck*'s speed was reduced, which in the C-in-C's view led to the enemy being brought to action. The next day there was no sign of the quarry. The search continued until 2230 on 26 May, when a Catalina made a sighting. A strike of 14 Swordfish was launched from *Ark Royal*, but returned without success. That evening another strike of 15 aircraft from 810, 818, and 826 squadrons launched from *Ark*, and obtained two certain hits, one of which damaged propellers and jammed the rudders. *Bismarck*'s fate was sealed. She was eventually dispatched, colours flying, by a torpedo from the cruiser HMS *Dorsetshire*.

BACK TO THE MEDITERRANEAN

On 13 November 1941, *Ark Royal* was torpedoed and sunk after making her eleventh ferry run to Malta. However, her squadron of 812 Swordfish with ASV, operating from Gibraltar, in three weeks damaged five U-boats, forcing them to return to base for repairs, and sank *U451*, the first submarine to be destroyed, at night, by aircraft.

There was no carrier operational in the Eastern Mediterranean from May 1941 to December 1942, after the withdrawal of *Illustrious* and *Formidable* with extensive battle damage. The FAA, however, continued to be operationally successful in the area, at sea and on the land. 815 Squadron from *Illustrious*, after spells in Greece and Crete, undertook anti-shipping and A/S work in Libya and Egypt. In 1942 they specialised in night A/S strikes using ASV. They attacked over 30 U-boats, badly damaged three and sank one, contributing to a marked decrease in allied shipping losses.

821 and 826 Squadrons flying Albacores perfected their techniques of night bombing the Africa Corps in 1942. Navigating over featureless desert to a

The Albacore three-seat TBR, ordered in 1937, entered service in March 1940. Its main advantages over the Swordfish it was designed to replace, were crew comfort, enclosed cockpits and heating, but it lacked the agility and manoeuvrability of its predecessor, which continued in production. The crew cockpit featured a rear-hinged canopy from which the Air Gunner Telegraphist could fire his machine gun, which was recessed in the rear fuselage

map reference, they adopted a flare-dropping pattern which the RAF later developed in its Pathfinder force. With the bottom of the Albacore's wings painted black, and the propeller in coarse pitch to reduce noise, two aircraft would illuminate the target with flares while the rest of the squadron attacked with 250 lb bombs. The army greatly appreciated their accuracy.

Then came the idea of co-operating with the RAF to drop a heavier weight of bombs. The Albacores would illuminate the target for an hour, and the RAF Wellingtons would bomb through the flares on large targets such as airfields and concentrations of transport and supplies.

MALTA

The strike activities of the FAA squadrons stationed in Malta played an essential part in the North Africa campaign, intercepting and destroying convoys carrying supplies, bombing enemy ports in North Africa and Sicily, and minelaying.

In 1941, 830 Squadron Swordfish were equipped with long-range tanks and one aircraft fitted with ASV. Their technique was for the strike leader to carry flares and bombs, to illuminate the target found by ASV, and the rest of the formation to attack with torpedoes. In October, the Albacores of 828 Squadron joined them.

By January 1942, Field Marshall Kesselring had arrived to organise the blitz on Malta. 8,000 tons of bombs were dropped between February and April. By June only one Swordfish remained serviceable. The air attacks on Malta eased by September and the FAA was able to step up its attacks when replacement aircraft were flown in. The 'Malta boys' eventually sank a total of 250,000 tons of enemy shipping.

THE BATTLE OF THE ATLANTIC

The U-boat's ascendancy in the North Atlantic was reaching a critical point in 1942; 1,700 allied ships, totalling 8 million tons, had been lost. Convoys were the answer but had to be provided with continuous air cover. The use of Fleet Carriers would be a waste of resources and something smaller, which could operate as part of the convoy, was required. Escort Carriers were to be the answer, carrying two squadrons: Swordfish for A/S and Martlets for fighter escort. They were introduced in 1941, but faults in the aviation fuel system delayed their effective use until April 1943.

In the meantime, during 1943, the MAC ships were introduced (eventually 19 of them). The Merchant Aircraft Carriers were grain ships, or oil tankers, fitted with flight decks and operating four Swordfish. They could carry 90% of their normal cargo with aircraft embarked. They did not sink any U-boats, but no convoy with a MAC ship ever lost a vessel.

Describing the A/S Swordfish sorties, Hugh Popham, in his book *Into Wind* says "To the airmen peering hour after hour for a periscope wake or the black amorphous outline of a surfaced U-boat, or the blip on an ASV screen, no convoy could be more disagreeable, more dangerous than another; but the quality they all shared was the feeling of interminability."

Navigation was often a problem. Low cloud or fog made it difficult to find an accurate wind. Signals of changes in course and speed of the convoy often failed to reach the aircraft. What crews hated most was a patrol astern of the convoy. Overtaking a convoy could be a grim struggle. During one voyage two MAC ships were in company when a Swordfish, returning from astern, experienced a head wind of 60 knots, reducing its ground speed to 20 knots. Radar operators on the ships watched the blip on the screen until it faded out. Its fuel exhausted, the plane was never seen again.

By September 1944 the Escort Carriers were transferred to offensive operations off Norway. The Battle of the Atlantic was won.

THE LAST LAP

During 1944, Fleet and Escort carriers operated Barracudas, Fireflies, and Avengers off the coast of Norway. They attacked shipping with bombs, torpedoes, rockets, and mines, causing more damage in the area than any other part of the Royal Navy or the RAF.

The Fairey Barracuda, three-seat torpedo-bomber reconnaissance aircraft. Entering service in January 1943, these aircraft dive-bombed Tirpitz in April 1944. 42 aircraft scored 15 direct hits with armour-piercing bombs

Fairey Firefly I. Designed as a two-seat fighter, the first squadron formed up in October1943 and its first operational sortie was to escort the Barracudas attacking the Tirpitz. A secondary role was strike reconnaissance, but soon the addition of rocket projectiles made it a true strike aircraft

Grumman Avenger. It served from 1943, mostly as a bomber and strike aircraft with R/Ps

The Normandy landings, in June 1944, were supported by the FAA from airfields on the South coast with shipping strikes and A/S patrols. These were backed up by radar-equipped Swordfish.

Two-seat Swordfish III. This was equipped with improved Mk 10 ASV radar which had an all-round display showing coastline and shipping

By 1943 the intake of aircrew had reached 200 per month. In 1944, the Admiralty realised there was an excess of newly-trained aircrew, particularly observers, and half of 66 Observers Course were allowed to opt for pilot training. Some were sent to MTBs as navigation or signals officers. On D-day many qualified 'Os' were used as Beach Signals Officers, or as liaison officers with the RAF and USAAF.

THE FAR EAST

In the Far East the full potential of the FAA was to be tried and tested. The Eastern Fleet was split into the British Pacific Fleet and the East Indies Fleet in 1944. The former, used in the main offensive against Japan; the latter to support the 14th army in Burma and sever supply lines to garrisons in outlying islands. By August 1945 the Eastern Fleet had 16 assault or strike carriers. The BPF operated with a nucleus of four fleet carriers, which were supplied with replacement aircraft by five escort carriers.

The aircrew, whose average age was 21, had been trained for war in the Far East. They were faced with the problems of operating large formations of aircraft, in particular, rendezvousing before and after attacks with aircraft of differing speeds and endurance. The problems were exacerbated by flight-deck delays. Nevertheless, the FAA proved to be a highly mobile, efficient, and hard-hitting force, capable of engaging and defeating the enemy over its own territory. The Firefly was shown to be the most formidable all-weather strike aircraft in the FAA, and ship-for-ship, the British had kept up the same rate of striking as the Americans.

AIRCRAFT PERFORMANCE DETAILS

Aircraft	Role Crew	In Service	Speed	Range	Armament
Swordfish 2392	TBR 2/3	1936	100 kts	450 nm	2 mg, 1 torp or 1,500 lb-bombs D/Cs, rockets.
Skua 182	F/B 2	1938	196 kts	767 nm	5 mg, 500 lb-bombs
Albacore 800	TBR 3	1940	150 kts	550 nm	2 mg, 1 torp or 2,000 lb of a/s stores
Fulmar 600	F/R 2	1940	231 kts	680 nm	8 mg, 2 x 250 lb bombs
Barracuda 2572	TBR 3	1943	150 kts	596 nm	2 mg, 1,500 lb of stores
Avenger 958	TBR 3	1943	232 kts	983 nm	5 mg, 1 torp, 2,000 lb of stores
Firefly 870	F/R 2	1943	277 kts	671 nm	4 cannon, 1,000 lb of stores, 8 rockets

POST WAR DEVELOPMENTS

2 September 1945. VJ Day: All classes of aircraft carrier 59. Home air stations 68, Overseas 37.

Within a year, 59 front line squadrons were disbanded. Most of the RNVR aircrew returned to civilian life. Those that remained exchanged their wavy stripes for straight ones, under a short service scheme, which revived the RN (A) branch. Permanent RN and RM officers could still specialise as aircrew.

In 1946, advised by the Godden Committee, their Lordships decided to stop training observers and to rely, in future, on single-seat aircraft. Some of the observers who had volunteered for the short service scheme found themselves on a pilot's course, or accepted a short service commission as an Air Traffic Controller. Others continued to practise their skills in the Sea Hornet NF21 (809 Squadron), and as strike or A/S in Firefly 5s and 6s (820, 814, 824 Squadrons).

On 18 October 1945 there were 182 practising observers, which by 22 February 1946 were dropped to 61.

Sea Hornet NF 21, with improved AI radar. From 1949 to 1954 it was the only front-line night fighter

The formation of NATO (North Atlantic Treaty Organisation), in 1949, in response to a perceived threat from the Communist bloc, led to the reassessment of the need for observers, so that Britain could carry out her commitments. An eight-year short service commission was offered to candidates with suitable qualifications, to supplement volunteers from RM and RN officers. They would receive a gratuity at the end of their service and could be offered a permanent commission. Entries were arranged in January, April, July and October.

Initial training of six months took place in the training carrier, and included seamanship, W/T, naval etiquette, and sea experience in other types of naval vessel. This was followed by six months flying training at RNAS St Merryn (Cornwall) in Ansons, Barracudas, and Firefly Is, learning and practising air navigation, radar homings, and W/T. The training was completed at RNAS Eglinton (Northern Ireland) with a two month A/S course, continuing with air navigation, radar detection and homings, W/T, and the use of passive sonobuoys. A pattern of five buoys would be dropped on the last known position of a submerged submarine, determining its course and position with reference to the strength of the noise of the cavitation from its propellers, picked up by the buoys. The information was then passed to an approaching A/S Frigate.

National Service ratings could volunteer for aircrew as long as they agreed to join the RNVR Squadrons after qualifying. These squadrons flew at weekends and did a two-week annual refresher course at sea.

In 1955 the targets for Observer training were:

Short Service Commission 60

National Service   20

Fleet Entry   10

The Director of Naval Recruitment commented: "Concern over the recruitment of observers is due to the complete lack of publicity. The role of observers in modern jet fighter/strike aircraft should be emphasised." He recommended that: "Any time between four and eight years from entry, a proportion of officers should be given the opportunity to volunteer for permanent commissions. If short service commissions were not attractive enough to encourage more observers, compulsory specialisation from General Service should be considered." (Shades of the 1930s)

A replacement Firefly 5 being hoisted aboard HMS Glory at Iwakuni in southern Japan

THE KOREAN WAR

In the meantime, the FAA was to be called into action when North Korean forces invaded South Korea in June 1950. The Light Fleet Carriers, *Triumph*, *Glory*, and *Ocean*, served consecutively alongside the American Fleet until July 1953.

Once again two-seat aircraft were to prove their worth at mine-laying and in A/S and Fighter/Strike/Reconnaissance roles. Firefly Is of 827 Squadron were soon to be replaced by Firefly 5s, also operated by 810, 812, and 825 Squadrons.

Michael Apps, an observer in 812, operating from HMS *Glory*, described the situation in 1952:

"A full scale effort of air strikes was ordered to destroy and batter enemy supply trains, blow up ammunition dumps, sink junks, sampans and barges, strafe enemy troops and gun emplacements, and generally to create as much havoc as possible.

"The North Koreans were past masters in the art of camouflage, and had an astonishing aptitude for improvisation in keeping land communications running, and supplies moving. The Chinese and North Koreans maintained a nightly flow of traffic by both rail and road, which was supplemented by horses, mules, camels, ox-carts, and coolie power, using tracks and trails over the mountains.

"I was in a flight of four Fireflies ordered to strike a tunnel in which an ammunition train was hiding. After successfully bombing and blocking both ends of the tunnel, we bagged two ox-carts on the way home, dispersed liberal quantities of 20mm cannon fire at gun emplacements and wandering communist soldiery, landing safely back on board some two hours later."

By the end of the war, squadrons had brought their efficiency to new heights and were the subject of many congratulatory signals from both American and British High Commands.

814 Squadron Firefly A/S6 on the lift of HMS Eagle, 1953

NEW TASKS – NEW AIRCRAFT

The last operational development of the Firefly was the A/S 6, with the omission of cannon and provision for the carriage and monitoring of British sonobouys. The first front-line squadron to receive the aircraft was 814, in January 1951, which with 809 Squadron (Sea Hornets) formed the 7th Night Air Group, the FAA's first all-weather unit. 814 completed 927 hours night flying during 1951, recognised by the award of the Boyd Trophy. In March 1954, Grumman Avengers replaced their A/S 6s, to bridge the gap before the arrival of the Fairey Gannet.

The De Havilland Sea Venom replaced the Sea Hornet in 1954, carrying the first jet-propelled observer in a purpose-built, all-weather fighter (FAW). Capable at night (or in cloud) of successful interceptions at 40,000 ft, with a pick up range on other Venoms of 12 miles, FAW 20s were flown by 890, 809, and 891 Squadrons, using AI 10 radar.

Training was initially with the RAF. Part one (two months) was at RAF Colerne in Brigand IVs, and part two (three months) was at RAF Leeming in Meteor NF 11s. Handfuls of younger observers were being appointed to these courses, which left many front-line squadrons undermanned.

Late in 1955, 766 Squadron was being used as a holding unit for observers trained on the RAF Venom NF 3 at North Luffenham using AI 21, the radar in the newly forming Sea Venom FAW 21 squadrons, with a pick up range of 16 miles. 766 Squadron started its role as the FAW Training Unit in early 1956.

De Havilland Sea Venom FAW 21

Basic observer training had been transferred to RNAS Culdrose in 1954, with 750 Squadron flying Sea Prince T1s and Firefly T7s. The first three months were spent in the back of Sea Princes with an instructor teaching the student how to navigate, how to operate the radar, and to maintain W/T communications. During the following six months the students put into practice techniques taught on the ground and in the air, in day and night exercises in the Fireflies.

The Gannet A/S1 went front line with 826 NAS in January 1955. The first RN aircraft to seek and destroy submarines; its all-round radar housed in a retractable dustbin in the rear of the fuselage (observer please retract before landing) would pick up the target, and sonobuoys track it under water. The bomb bay was capable of carrying two homing torpedoes, or mines, depth charges, or bombs. In addition, rockets could be carried under the wings. 172 A/S1s were built. In August 1956, the first A/S4s, 90 of which were produced, joined 824 NAS. The last fixed wing front line A/S squadron was disbanded in July 1960.

Gannet A/S 1s, taking off and landing on HMS Albion, 1956, 825 NAS

AIRBORNE EARLY WARNING

A completely new role for the FAA was AEW. The first aircraft to be used in this capacity was the Douglas Skyraider, fitted with the General Electric AN/APS 20 radar. It carried two observers who were able to detect air and sea forces and to direct counter attacks many miles from the fleet. A medium-sized aircraft could be detected at a range of 50 miles.

In July 1952, at RNAS Culdrose, 849 NAS was reformed with AEW Skyraiders. The Headquarters (Training) Flight stationed at the parent airfield detached separate Flights A, B, C, and D, to various carriers. Fifty Skyraiders were to be purchased by the RN.

HMS Bulwark 849, 'D' Flight AEW Skyraider

To elaborate on the roles of the Skyraider; the primary function was to guard against low-flying attackers and shadowers, reporting contacts and directing friendly fighters to deal with the threat. Similar functions were carried out with A/S aircraft being directed to possible submarine contacts (periscope or snorkel contacts in suitable sea conditions) and strike direction for air attacks on enemy surface vessels. However, for the ship's company, the most popular role was the 'Wells Fargo' operation: the collection and delivery of mail, the flying ashore of compassionate cases and, for the operational efficiency of the ship and aircraft, the collection of spares. There was no shortage of 849 aircrew volunteers to man these jaunts, which often resulted in a night or two ashore ahead of the ship.

INTO BATTLE – SUEZ

In July 1956, President Nasser nationalised the Suez Canal. In co-operation with the French, an attack on Egypt was planned by the British Government with the object of securing the canal. Code named Operation Musketeer, its aim was to secure our trade from the East, particularly in oil. Ground based aircraft were out of range of the combat area, except for heavy bombers. The FAA, therefore, provided strikes to destroy the Egyptian aircraft on the ground, attacked military installations and covered the troop landings.

Observer-manned aircraft included five Sea Venom strike squadrons; Gannets carried out A/S patrols, and Skyraiders AEW cover for the joint fleets, as well as providing ship-to-shore communications and stores flights. It was found that by removing one of the observer's seats it was possible to load over 1,000 cans of beer into the rear cabin – much to the delight of the troops ashore. The FAA carried out its tasks exceptionally well but because of American political pressure a cease-fire was negotiated.

RNVR

In 1946 the Admiralty decided to re-form the RNVR flying units and, in 1947, the first (1830 Squadron) was formed at RNAS Abbotsinch for A/S duties. The RNVR Air Branch was expanded, particularly on the A/S side, beginning in 1951. Eventually a further five A/S squadrons were formed and, together with the fighter squadrons, the final total strength was eleven squadrons.

The A/S squadrons operated progressive marks of Firefly up to the A/S 6, as well as Avengers, and the Channel Air Division re-equipped with Gannets in 1956. The following year the RNVR Air Divisions were disbanded. The observer with the most hours in nearly five years was Lt W Almond RNVR, with close to 500.

LEARNING FROM EXPERIENCE

The following extract is taken from an article in *Fly Navy*, written by Lt R D McCulloch RN. Observer, 894 Squadron, HMS *Eagle*, Moray Firth 1957.

"I was airborne on 9 August in one of a pair of Sea Venom FAW 22s, practising radar intercepts, when the weather suddenly closed in. The only way of getting back on deck was going to be a Carrier Controlled Approach, Air Traffic Controllers using the ship's radar to talk us down until we were close enough to see the deck and [to] land. The ship's radar was not designed for such close range work on a small, fast-moving target, and we saw nothing of the ship on our first approach. Next time round we were advised to look for the mirror, *Eagle*'s 150ft superstructure flashed past our left wing tip in the fog. It should have been on the other side. We were told to divert to RAF Kinloss.

"Although equipped with precision GCA radar, the operators, used to dealing with one or two slow moving Shackletons, found eight Navy jets (short of fuel and clamouring for immediate landing in marginal weather) another kettle of fish. We decided to do our own approach. Using the sharp coastal echo on my

AI-21 radar, I conned the pilot down below cloud over the sea into a bay towards the western end of Kinloss's east-west runway. After a very tight circuit we managed to put the aircraft on the concrete before the engine stopped."

In *Eagle* the incident stimulated some lateral thinking by the CO and Senior Observer of 894. Use the Sea Venom radar, which was designed to track small contacts, for Carrier Controlled Approach. "Back on board I soon found myself sitting in a Sea Venom, parked facing aft behind the island, using my radar to talk down a couple of Venoms on simulated CCAs." The trial was a great success, and a special shack was built just aft of the island to house an AI-21 radar, which was soon fitted to all fixed-wing carriers.

HELICOPTERS

The RN was the first service to order helicopters for operational use, in 1943. The first naval helicopter squadron was formed in 1947 and extensive ship-borne trials were started in 1951. Soon Westland Dragonflies were being used in the air-sea rescue role as plane guards for carriers, and also for sea rescue around the British Isles. In 1953, the author was able to appreciate the effectiveness of the Dragonfly after ditching in a Firefly 6 of 814 Squadron and being returned by the plane guard to HMS *Eagle*.

The next important development for observers was the adoption of the larger Whirlwind for A/S duties. The Whirlwind HAS 7 was equipped with a dipping or 'dunking' sonar device. 845 Squadron was the first front line unit to take it to sea, in HMS *Bulwark*, in 1957. The Gannet began to be replaced by the Whirlwind in A/S squadrons but, due to engine transmission troubles, it did not become the standard A/S aircraft until 1960.

Whirlwind HAS 7 being used for A/S aircrew training, at RNAS Culdrose, by 706 Squadron

TANKER SALVAGE

On September 13, 1958, HMS *Bulwark* was exercising with the frigate HMS *Loch Killisport* in the Gulf of Oman. At 0718, she received the following signal from the tanker Anglian Diligence: "Liberian tanker Melika in collision with French tanker Fernand Gilabert." The position given was 150 miles south of *Bulwark*, which proceeded at 23 knots towards the collision area.

The disabled Fernand Gilabert

The Search

A 'D' Flight Skyraider was sent to search in the reported position and reached the scene of the collision at 0840. She saw a tanker, which could not be immediately identified, on fire forward, belching black smoke and down at the bow. There was no sign of the second tanker. A relief Skyraider, flown by

Lt Bob Creasy RN, identified the burning tanker as the Fernand Gilabert and it was photographed by Lt Keith Davies RN.

Just before midday, *Bulwark*'s two doctors were flown ahead by 845 Squadron helicopters to give medical aid to casualties recovered to the rescue ships. Two more helicopters ferried Cdr Brunner RN, and a small fire-fighting team to the Fernand Gilabert, where they set about getting the fires under control. Other helicopters ferried the injured from the rescue ships to *Bulwark*.

Reports from the rescue ships had indicated that, after being abandoned, the Melika had continued to steam south. At 1400 a searching Skyraider reported her stopped, on fire amidships, and listing, 25 miles south of *Bulwark*. Another fire-fighting party was lowered onto the forecastle of the burning ship by helicopters of 845 NAS.

Bulwark then steamed towards Masira Island to fly off three helicopters and a Skyraider to take seriously injured survivors to RAF Masira, the Skyraider acting as navigational shepherd for the helicopters. The injured landed at Masira were later flown to Bahrein by the RAF.

During the afternoon of 14 September, the first attempt to pass a tow to Melika from *Bulwark* was unsuccessful. During the forenoon of the next day *Loch Killisport* reported that she had successfully taken Fernand Gilabert in tow and they were proceeding towards Karachi at three knots. In the afternoon *Bulwark* commenced the tow of the Melika.

The stricken Melika

An essential task was to restore power in the tanker as, without steam for the capstan, all the working of the heavy chain cable and the large wires had to be done by hand. Before restoring power, the boilers, which were in a dreadful state, required cleaning. Volunteers, mainly aircrew officers from *Bulwark*, spent many hours below, where it was extremely hot and indescribably filthy. Many afterwards proudly displayed stoker's badges on their flying suits.

On 17th September, 1958, a Skyraider was launched by free take-off from Bulwark. The first time a carrier towing a ship had operated fixed wing aircraft

The next day ship handling proved a little easier when power steering became available in Melika. The following morning, 19 September, Melika was anchored off Muscat, and a signal was received that the Fernand Gilabert had safely reached Karachi.

Bulwark had earned the largest, and the last, salvage prize ever won by one of HM ships – £100,000, much to the delight of her crew who each received an appropriate share.

A NEW ERA

In 1958 the FAA was on the threshold of a new era, with the prospect of new high performance aircraft having advanced weaponry and better methods of detection, in the air, and under water.

The Sea Vixen, replacement for the Sea Venom, came into service in July 1959 when 892 Squadron was formed at Yeovilton. The AI 18 developed for the Vixen had a pick-up range of up to 32 miles on another Vixen, and fed into the new 984 radar system on the carriers. This system fed displays in the operations room, linking early warning aircraft radar to the plots, thus giving an overall picture of the position and height of aircraft in any sector of the sky. The Vixen FAW1 had no guns. It was armed with Firestreak air-to-air missiles and Bull Pup air-to-surface missiles. The FAW2, introduced in 1963, carried Red Top air-to-air missiles and also had a nuclear capability. Longer tail booms extended ahead of the wing leading edges, to carry more fuel, and a refuelling probe was fitted. As well as receiving fuel it could also refuel other aircraft.

Sea Vixen FAW 1 on the catapult

The Observer School moved to Malta in October 1959, where weather conditions permitted a better training environment. The following July, 750 Squadron took delivery of Sea Venoms for high-level navigation training. Observers training exercises would take them to Naples, Palma, and Rome. In the same year, 1960, initial naval training for Os was moved to RNC Britannia, Dartmouth, with a course entry of eight cadets.

By 1960 the number of Naval Air Stations had been reduced to 9 and Operational Carriers to 7.

'B' Flight AEW Gannet on the deck of Ark Royal

The AEW Gannet became operational in 1960, taking over from the Skyraider in 849 Squadron and using the AN/APS-20E. The radar picture could be sent back to the carrier by the relay known as 'Bellhop'.

Developed from the A/S Gannet, the AEW version had a larger, redesigned, fuselage to house the radar and scanner, plus a new tail section for better stability. An uprated Double Mamba provided the power. Forty-four AEW 3s were ordered and the squadron still operated in flights of four aircraft.

The Wessex was the world's first front-line helicopter to be powered by a gas turbine engine. This powerful unit nearly doubled the range, and enabled it to carry a greater payload than the Whirlwind. It was also the first ASW helicopter capable of night and all-weather dipping sonar operations, being equipped with an auto stabiliser. This allowed the aircraft to remain at a constant height above sea level. Crew: two pilots and an observer. 815 Squadron commissioned with the Wessex HAS 1 at Culdrose on 4 July 1961.

In 1967, the improved HAS 3 came into service with radar, improved sonar and flight control systems, and an uprated engine. These helicopters operated from carriers, guided missile County Class destroyers, and the cruiser HMS *Blake*.

Wessex HAS 3

The Buccaneer was arguably the best aircraft ever procured for the RN. The world's first specialised low-level strike aircraft, it proved outstanding in its intended role. The Buccaneer S1 became operational with 801 Squadron at Lossiemouth in 1962 before embarking in *Ark Royal*. Upgraded in 1964 to the S2, it was capable of carrying a nuclear bomb in addition to more conventional weapons. Provision was also made for photo-reconnaissance. The crew of pilot and observer had the benefit of a sophisticated navigational package. Doppler navigation linked to the Decca roller map, and Airpass air-to-surface radar, provided ground mapping, conventional radar ranging and terrain warning modes of operation. This, integrated with a strike sight, provided the pilot with information via a head-up display unit and the observer with his display.

The Buccaneer made use of a special bomb release known as LABS (Low Altitude Bombing System). It was designed to allow the safe delivery of a nuclear bomb by ensuring the aircraft was not consumed in its own nuclear fireball: after a high speed, low-level approach it pulled up at three miles

Buccaneer S2. Note the probe for receiving fuel and refuelling other aircraft. Two Rolls Royce Speys, providing a 30% increase in thrust and a range of 3,000 miles at Mach .85, replaced the original De Havilland Gyron engines

and, at 45° nose up, 'tossed' the bomb on to the target, completing the half loop and exiting fast in the opposite direction as low as possible. Weapon release was timed by computer, the observer's job being to get to the release point at the right speed, height and climb angle.

The Westland Wasp was designed to operate from the deck of frigates to augment their A/S capabilities. Guided by the mother ship's sonar it could

The Westland Wasp

attack the target with homing torpedoes, depth charges, or two AS12 wire-guided missiles. Operationally it carried a two-man crew, but in its light communications role could also carry three passengers.

The first Leander-type frigate was delivered in 1963. In March 1964, 829 Squadron was formed at Culdrose, as the parent squadron for the Wasp helicopters operating from these ships. In November, the squadron moved to RNAS Portland which had been opened as an operational training unit base for A/S helicopter crews since 1959.

Observer Recruitment

Although the total observer strength was approaching 200, supply was still not keeping up with the demand for crewing new aircraft. In 1963, a Buccaneer crew were seconded to give recruitment talks to Combined Cadet Force units, but finding observers was still a problem in 1964. This was attributed to a misunderstanding, or ignorance, of the role of the observer. The RAF was a more attractive flying prospect, with more modern aircraft, and less difficult for a married man, who would not have to undertake long operational tours at sea. The recruitment brochures of the 'Silent Service' perhaps should have mentioned that flying training was based in Malta.

CARRIERS AND AIR STATIONS

By 1960, the last of the wartime carriers had been broken up or sold to other navies. HMS *Bulwark* was recommissioned and converted to the commando role, equipped to carry helicopters and a Royal Marine Commando unit, to be closely followed by HMS *Albion*. A new large carrier, the CVA-01, had been announced in 1963 but was cancelled in 1966. This signalled the end of conventional carriers, with long flight decks, capable of launching and landing high performance fixed wing aircraft.

The Phantom, ordered from the USA in 1963 to replace the Vixen, was delivered to RNAS Yeovilton in 1968. The original order of 200 was whittled down to 28 following the decision to run down the carrier force. The new carriers (Through deck cruisers) would be smaller vessels designed to operate helicopters and V/STOL (Vertical short take-off and landing) Sea Harriers.

Phantom FG1. Crew: Pilot and Observer. At this time, it was the RN's only supersonic aircraft

Eagle, Ark Royal, Victorious, Centaur and *Hermes* continued to carry out the more traditional roles. The carriers and their squadrons were tasked in Kuwait (under threat from Iraq) in 1961. Borneo was threatened by Indonesia in 1962, the Rhodesian crisis occurred in 1965 and Arab insurrections in Yemen and Aden in 1967.

Meanwhile, in 1964, the Observer School and 750 Squadron returned from Malta and took up residence at RNAS Lossiemouth. There were still overseas navigational flights, on a reduced scale, to places including Amsterdam, Copenhagen, Brussels, and Oslo. At the same time, 849 AEW Squadron moved from RNAS Culdrose to RNAS Brawdy.

The Sea King, a new and powerful helicopter, took to the air in 1969. This twin-engine, all-weather aircraft was primarily designed for the detection, identification, and destruction of enemy submarines. It was a self-contained tactical unit, with integrated radar and sonics display. Underwater tracking of submarines was achieved by a passive system using sonobuoys and an active system using dipping sonar (see glossary). The Sea King had a comprehensive armoury, including homing torpedoes, depth bombs and guided missiles, with which to attack submarines and also surface vessels. It was to operate from carriers, cruisers, and later, destroyers. In February 1970, the first front-line Sea King Squadron, 824, was commissioned at RNAS Culdrose.

Sea King HAS 1

The 1970s

849 Squadron again found itself on the move in 1970, when HQ Flight transferred to Lossiemouth from Brawdy. Both air stations were to be taken over by the RAF. In 1972, the 'O' School moved from Lossiemouth to Culdrose where, in 1976, 750 Squadron's ancient Sea Princes began to be replaced by Jetstream T2s.

Jetstream T2. Used as a flying classroom for navigation and radar training

In the meantime, *Ark Royal* emerged from a major refit and, in 1970, became the most powerful strike weapon the FAA had ever possessed, with her

Phantoms, Buccaneers, AEW Gannets and A/S Sea Kings. Other carriers were rapidly disappearing. *Eagle* was scrapped in 1972, *Albion* in 1973, and *Bulwark* went into reserve in 1976. Then *'Ark'* was scrapped in 1978 and her Phantoms and Buccaneers were handed over to the RAF. AEW was finished and 849 disbanded, though some of the radar sets were installed in ancient Shackletons, a token of the RAF's commitment to the defence of the fleet.

Thus at the Falklands, in 1982, the powerful strike a/c were not available to attack the Argentine Fleet and support the ground forces. The Gannets were to be sorely missed from the defence of the fleet, with their ability to detect ships at 180 miles, reconnaissance a/c at 90 miles, and fighters approaching head on (at low level) at 60 miles. Their two observers could have simultaneously directed fighter interceptions, and strikes on ships and land targets.

HMS *Hermes* still remained, having been converted to a Commando Carrier in 1973. Then, in 1979, HMS *Invincible* a 'Through Deck Cruiser', looking remarkably like an aircraft carrier, did her sea trials and was commissioned in the following year with squadrons of A/S Sea Kings and Sea Harriers.

Lynx HAS 2, armed with a torpedo

The demise of the carriers had led to the requirement for a new helicopter to undertake ship-borne duties. Designed and built by Westland, the Lynx first flew in 1971. Sixty modified HAS 2s were delivered to the Royal Navy in the late 1970s. They were tasked to carry out reconnaissance, also attacks on submarines, using homing torpedoes, and on surface vessels, using Sea Skua missiles.

THE 1980s

In October, 1980, Saddam Hussein (in Iraq) and Ayatollah Khomeini (in Iran) fell out over the Shatt-al-Arab. Iraq then invaded Iran. America sent ships to the Persian Gulf to protect the tanker routes. The British provided the Armilla Patrol. This naval squadron consisted of two destroyers and two frigates supported by an RFA tanker and a stores ship in the Gulf, outside the Straits of Hormuz.

Sea King modifications. The HAS 5 became operational in 1981. Its Decca Sea Searcher radar, having double the range of the Echo system on the HAS 1, needed a noticeably larger dorsal radome. The dipping sonar could detect a submarine at up to eight nautical miles range.

By the mid 1980s, it was apparent that a sensor upgrade was required. The HAS 6 was ordered in 1987 and, fitted with new sonar processing equipment and improved tracking devices, was delivered to 820 NAS in January 1990.

Sea King HAS 5

THE FALKLANDS AIR WAR

Argentinian forces occupied Port Stanley on 2 April, 1982. On 3 April, Prime Minister Mrs Thatcher approved the creation of a task force to recapture the Falkland Islands. The first enemy aircraft to be sighted was a Boeing 707, shadowing the Fleet as it approached the Islands on the 25 April. On the same day, Royal Navy ships, HMS *Antrim*, HMS *Plymouth*, RFA *Tydespring*, and HMS *Endurance*, arrived off South Georgia to deal with the Argentinian force which had landed there.

The SAS, against expert advice, insisted on being inserted on the Fortuna Glacier, which was to put the whole operation in jeopardy. *Antrim*'s Wessex 3 led the two Wessex 5s from *Tydespring*, carrying the SAS, using radar to home on to the glacier. The first attempt failed, but the second was successful in spite of marginal weather. That night, 21/22 April, the troops radioed their position was untenable. The three helicopters reached the glacier safely. YF was first to take off in white-out conditions, and was seen to crash. The other two lifted and landed next to the crashed aircraft to embark survivors. 406 returned to *Antrim*, but YS flared violently over a ridge, and rolled on its side. After debarking his troops, 406 returned to rescue the last remaining survivors from the wreck of YS.

During 24/25 April, it was reported that the Argentinian submarine *Santa Fe* might attempt to enter Grytviken. It was decided to launch *Antrim*'s Wessex for a surface search/ASW sortie. The area of Cumberland Bay was searched visually. With one sweep of the Wessex radar carried out, a tiny echo was detected at 5 nm and recognised as the submarine at one mile. It was immediately attacked with depth charges and headed for Grytviken, pouring oil and smoke. *Brilliant*'s Lynx then attacked the sub with a Mark 46 torpedo and closed to engage it with a GPMG (General Purpose Machine Gun) until *Plymouth*'s Wasp delivered an AS12 from 40 miles under the control of *Antrim*'s Wessex. The submarine was subsequently abandoned.

Lt Cdr I Stanley RN – Awarded The DSO

The Flight Commander of HMS *Antrim* flew seven sorties in the course of two days to rescue the men of the reconnaissance party and the crews of the crashed helicopters...in snowstorms...gale force winds...and also contributed to a marked degree to the successful attack on...the Argentine submarine *Santa Fe*.

Let's hope his observer got a congratulatory pat on the back.

26 April – After a hurried conference, the Task Group Commander decided to go ahead with the assault on South Georgia. At 1445, *Antrim*'s Wessex led *Brilliant*'s two Lynx to land troops after a demonstration bombardment. There was one enemy casualty.

27 April – Sea King 5s of 820 and 826 Squadrons began flying sector searches from HMS *Hermes* and HMS *Invincible* as a precaution against Argentine surface ship intervention and possible submarine attack. They also operated detachments from *Fort Austin, Atlantic Causeway*, and San Carlos in ASW and reconnaissance roles. They maintained a 24-hour A/S screen around the many ships of the Falklands Task Force.

Wessex, Lynx, and Wasps from the frigates reconnoitred the bays and inlets. The Lynx engaged surface targets with brand new Sea Skua missiles, scoring eight hits with eight firings, destroying one Argentine ship and seriously damaging two others. A Lynx detachment was made to each carrier to increase the punch available in surface actions. Decoy helicopters were fitted with radar reflectors to attract Exocet missiles away from the ship. They flew between the ship and the incoming missile, maintaining their safety by hovering above the height at which the Exocet was approaching.

On 2 May, the Command Briefing stated that the Argentine Fleet had put to sea. To the south the Exocet armed cruiser *General Belgrano* was being shadowed by the nuclear submarine HMS *Conqueror*. Lt Cdr Ward, the CO of 801 Squadron, suggested that a Sea Harrier be sent to the north west to find the other half of the pincer, the carrier task group containing the *Veinticinco de Mayo*. The plan was to fly 200 miles at high level, then cruise at low level for 40 miles before transmitting on radar. The Harrier flew off into the dark and followed the plan before the pilot switched on his radar at 40 miles. "I counted four ship contacts less than 25 miles away. The next thing I knew, all sorts of radar were illuminating me, including Sea Dart fire control, indicating they had at least one Type 42 out there." So the carrier was probably there too.

In the debrief, Wings observed that with little natural wind that night the Argentine carrier would have great difficulty launching its Skyhawks. It was known that the old steam catapult on the carrier *Veinticinco de Mayo* was in poor condition and underpowered. Without a strong wind the Skyhawks would be unable to get off the deck with a war load. The next day the *Belgrano* was sunk by the *Conqueror*. It was discovered later that the Argentine carrier had failed to find a wind for a launch and retired to the safety of the mainland shore, never to venture seawards again.

"The absence of AEW was a severe handicap," remarks the official report on the Falklands War. Far beyond the range of the RAF's ancient Shackletons, the effectiveness of the Navy's carriers was much reduced by having to keep out of the range of the low-level, Exocet-launching Super Etendards. Against these, with no AEW, there was no defence. Ships and many lives were lost as a result.

SHIPS and LIVES LOST IN ACTION

Date	Ship	Dead
4 May	HMS *Sheffield*	20
21 May	HMS *Ardent*	22
23 May	HMS *Antelope*	1
24 May	HMS *Coventry*	20
	Atlantic Conveyor	12
8 June	*Sir Galahad*	50

Sheffield and *Coventry* were sunk while specifically engaged in the out-of-date WWII task of forward radar picket duty. In monetary terms, AEW would have prevented the loss of at least £1,000 million.

In spite of having no AEW, air superiority was established and the Royal Marines and army were able to free the islands.

OBSERVERS' FLYING ACHIEVEMENT – Falkland Islands, April, May, June 1982

A/C Type + Mark	Squadrons	Hrs flown	No. of sorties
Sea King HAS 5	820, 826	6,489 hrs 30m	2,253
Wessex HAS 3	Antrim, Glamorgan Flights	333 hrs 25m	213
Lynx HAS 2	815	3,042 hrs 50m	4,405

14 June, Argentine Commander surrenders to the British.

Within 11 weeks of the surrender, a Sea King AEW 2 was fitted with a Thorne-EMI Searchwater radar, adapted from the type installed in the Nimrod MR2, as the main airborne sensor. The clutter rejection system was modified, providing detection of incoming anti-ship missiles and the ability to distinguish a snorkel from wave clutter at 10nm. The antenna, located in a starboard mounted Kevlar kettledrum fairing, lowered to the operational position when airborne. Two AEW Sea Kings, with Searchwater, sailed with 820 D Flight in HMS *Illustrious* for the South Atlantic.

Sea King AEW 2

In July 1982, the first Lynx HAS 3 with uprated engines and Seaspray search and tracking radar, installed in a modified nose-cone, was delivered to 815 Squadron.

Lynx HAS 3 with the modified nose-cone

REVISED OBSERVER TRAINING

By 1985 observer training had become helicopter orientated. After leaving Dartmouth, student observers joined a course group of 12 at 750 Squadron, Culdrose. The first month of the 27-week course with 750 was spent entirely in the classroom, studying basic navigation; meteorology; communications; the theory of instruments; airmanship; aerodynamics; principles of flight and ship recognition. Then followed further ground school plus 100 hours on Jetstreams, learning dead reckoning; low-level navigation; high-level navigation; wind finding; map reading and radar homings. Before sorties were attempted in the air, they were 'flown' by students in the Ground Trainer. This dramatically decreased the failure rate of 48% among students from four years before, to 8% in 1985.

After 750 Sqadron, the next stage for observers was 810 Squadron, except for those intended for Lynx Flights. 810 had been commissioned at RNAS Culdrose, in 1983, with 10 Sea King HAS 5s to train student pilots, observers,

810 Sea King HAS 5, operating a dipping sonar unit

and aircrewmen, through operational training to front-line status. Each course started with a group of 10 observers (8 A/S and 2 AEW) and, after five weeks on helicopter technique, the AEW observers progressed to 849 Squadron.

The ASW observers continued with AFT and gained their wings in 12 weeks. Then came a lengthy period of learning to control other aircraft and ships in the A/S war, to deliver weapons, and to fight the Sea King in active, and passive, search and attack. Secondary-role training was also undertaken in winching, flight refuelling, load carrying and search and rescue. Simulator training took place on the day before each sortie was flown. The course culminated in embarkation in the helicopter training ship HMS *Engadine.*

The young observer would then be appointed either to a carrier-based front-line squadron, or, perhaps, to the largest 826 Squadron, based at Culdrose. 826 had three flights each with five Sea King HAS 5s. Two of these flights would normally be detached to tankers and store ships of the Royal Fleet Auxiliary.

Training for Lynx observers took place with 702 Squadron at RNAS Portland. The lead-in phase was to familiarise them with the aircraft, flying at low level, and getting to grips with the computer. After 30 hours they went on to AFT: radar technology; coping with malfunctions; crewing up with their pilot and controlling sorties. At this time, they were also receiving intensive ground instruction in the operation of the weapons and equipment in the aircraft. The final phase, OFT, taught how to fight the Lynx: search techniques; weapon delivery; electronic warfare exercises; A/S warfare; fighter evasion; and air spotting for ship's gunnery.

Lynx helicopters were based on almost all frigates and destroyers by the mid 1980s. The observer would not only navigate and fight this multi-role helicopter, but also advise the command on using its most versatile weapon system to seek out and sink surface ships. The Lynx could find and destroy submarines, as well as keep electronic track of the enemy. It would jam the enemy's ability to do the same. The parenting squadron for the Lynx in 1986 was 829 Squadron, and the HQ Squadron was based at RNAS Portland.

The restoration of AEW at the end of the Falkland hostilities, by the formation of 824 D Flight, led to the re-formation of 849 Squadron in November 1984. After completing five weeks training with 810, the AEW students had six weeks at Yeovilton with basic instruction in Fighter Direction. They then returned to Culdrose for the Wings ceremony and a further 16 weeks training with 849. This included Combat Air Patrol Exercises, Electronic Counter Measures and Electronic Support Measures. Two observers operated side-by-side, picking up targets and directing the counter measures by ships and/or aircraft. When fully operational, 849 Squadron with eight AEW Sea Kings deployed two front-line flights (one in each operational carrier). Each flight had three aircraft, and five crews, with two training aircraft at Culdrose.

THE GULF CRISIS

In 1986, attacks on merchant shipping increased as the Iran/Iraq conflict escalated and many ships fell victim to the air-launched AM 39 Exocet. This led to the upgrading of the Lynx to HAS 3GM standard. The Yellow Veil jamming pod, and a fixed infrared jammer, were fitted to combat sophisticated infrared missiles used by the Iranian Revolutionary Guard. The Lynx, being flown from the two Armilla destroyers, were parented by 815 Squadron, and those from the frigates by 829 Sqadron, both based at Portland. Two Sea King HAS 5s from 826 D Flight, based at Culdrose, operated from RFA Olna.

With Iran exhausted, after eight years of war with Iraq, Saddam Hussein was becoming more confident. Kuwait and Saudi Arabia had obliged him by pumping oil above their OPEC quotas, depressing the world price and throttling Iran's only source of income. In 1990, Kuwait was trying to force Saddam into settling a long-standing border dispute in its favour by threatening him with his own cheap oil weapon. Believing the other Arab states were joining against him, Saddam demanded a payment of 10 million dollars to compensate for the low price of oil, to recoup his war losses and help Iraq's economic recovery. If this was not agreed to, he would invade Kuwait. On 3 August the Iraqi army invaded Kuwait. Britain immediately agreed to support America in rushing an army to Saudi Arabia to defend its oil, but it would take months before an effective force was assembled.

On 29 November, 1990, the UN Security Council voted twelve to two to "Call on member states co-operating with the government of Kuwait to use all necessary means to restore international peace and security, unless Iraq left Kuwait before January 15, 1991." The deadline passed without any agreement, and, with vastly superior forces in place, the allied air attack started at 0300 on 16 January, 1991.

Eight ships' flights were directly involved in the Gulf War, with British frigates, destroyers and RFAs operating in the north Persian Gulf. On 29 January, Lynx helicopters from HMS *Cardiff*, HMS *Gloucester* and HMS *Brazen*, in a joint operation with American forces, attacked 17 Iraqi small craft off the island of Maradin with Sea Skua missiles. One craft disappeared from the radar screen and it was later reported that four of the boats were seen beached on the coast. Lynx helicopters were also involved, as spotters, when the US Marines retook the Kuwait island of Qaruh.

Early on the morning of 11 February, a Lynx from HMS *Cardiff* scored a direct hit on a Soviet-built Zhuk fast patrol boat. It was the first British Lynx night engagement with the Iraqis. Almost 12 hours later, a Lynx from HMS *Manchester* attacked and destroyed an Iraqi coastal patrol boat. *Manchester* had only just arrived to relieve *Cardiff* in the Gulf.

Other ships in the area were HMS *Brave* and HMS *London*, operating with Lynx helicopters, and RFAs *Argus, Olna* and *Fort George,* with Sea Kings.

The allied land offensive 'Desert Storm' was launched on 24 February, defeating the Iraqi army in less than a week. On 3 March, an uneasy armistice was arranged and, apart from some occasional allied armed air 'policing' incursions. There was 'peace'.

1992 POLICY UPDATE

The First Sea Lord announced that the aim of the Navy Board was to preserve the Defence for the 90s Front Line policy. To this end a tender for a new helicopter carrier would be invited, and 44 Merlins had been ordered to replace Sea Kings in the anti-submarine role.

Lynx HAS 8

The development of the Lynx Mk 8 was nearing completion, and approval to update seven Lynx Mk 3s to Mk 8 standard had been received to meet an in-service date of December 1994. HAS 3s of 700L Squadron had conducted trials of the Lynx Central Tactical System, and new avionics, in the Caribbean. The CTS was to integrate the functions of the Radar, Sea Owl Passive Identification Device; Electronic Counter Measures; Electronic Surveillance Measures; the Navstar Global Positioning System; and Magnetic Anomaly Detector sensors. The Tactical Situation Display was to provide a colour picture of the tactical battle being fought and display navigational weapon status. The observer would control the input of the data displayed, manipulating the data to achieve the best results; perhaps the Chinagraph had been made redundant.

The most obvious external changes in the Mk 8 were in the reshaped nose, to accommodate the 360-degree radome, and the Sea Owl PID. The latter solving the problem of long-range target identification before weapon release. The first production Lynx Mk 8 of the Operational Evaluation Unit, 815 Squadron, made its inaugural deck landing on board the Duke class frigate, HMS *Montrose,* in 1995. By 1999 it was already serving in the smaller frigates, which were unable to accommodate larger helicopters.

CHANGES ASHORE

At the end of July 1993, 826 Squadron disbanded after 23 years continuous commission at Culdrose. The squadron's role of providing aircraft for small ship and RFA Flights was passed to 819 Squadron at Prestwick.

In 1994 RNAS Portland was closed. 829 Squadron was disbanded and 702 and 815 Squadrons transferred to Yeovilton.

By 1999 there were two female observers as part of aircrews and three more under training.

INTO THE 21st CENTURY

The year 2000 saw the introduction of the latest Lynx Mk 8, equipped with a Digital Signal Processor. It also saw the launch of an in-service degree scheme for RN aircrew. The 'Flying Start' scheme provides academic accreditation, through the Open University, of the training of RN aircrew. To obtain an OU degree it is necessary to gain 360 credit points (a significant amount of the points needed are accredited when the training is completed). The aircrew are then required to make up the gap through individual study from a range of modules. Depending on the student's choice, this can lead to the award of a general OU degree or to a degree in a named subject.

This scheme enables the young men and women to join the RN, as aircrew straight from school, and to earn credits from the moment they join Dartmouth.

The Merlin – In 2001, 824 Squadron was commissioned to train aircrew and engineers in every aspect of the Navy's new Merlin helicopter.

The most advanced anti-submarine and anti-surface helicopter in the world, the Merlin Mk 1 made its first official RN appearance on 1 Dec 1998, when 700M NAS commissioned at RNAS Culdrose. Larger, and faster, than the Sea King HAS 6 it replaces, it is as agile as the much smaller Lynx. Merlin has an extensive sensor package including a 360° radar; passive sonar processor and sonobuoy dispensing carousel; electronic support measures (radar detection) and a low frequency dipping sonar. It has a fully integrated tactical and secure communications system, data highway and linkage to

Merlin Mark 1

surface ships' action information systems, and is able to operate from the Type 23 frigates as well as aircraft carriers and auxiliaries.

At Culdrose, the 824 Merlin Training Facility provides computerised training in ground simulators for pilots, aircrew, and engineers. Three Rear Crew Trainers offer an exact replica of the Merlin cabin. When the ground training is completed the students move to the airborne syllabus, which includes navigation and radar, plus search and rescue techniques; then to operational tactics, including sonics, the datalink, stores and weapon systems. On completion of training, the students are ready to join a front line squadron.

814 NAS – The first front-line Merlin naval air squadron was formed in March 2001, having stood down as a Sea King squadron in December 2000. After working up at Culdrose, it joined the newly refitted HMS *Ark Royal* as the ASW element of the Carrier Air Group in May 2002.

A Sea King Mk 7 ASaC 'Cerberus', showing the Mk 2 dome on the spine replaced by an angular fitting above the cockpit

849 NAS, 2002 – A momentous year for the squadron, as it celebrates 50 years of AEW to the fleet with the introduction of the new Sea King Mk 7 Airborne Surveillance and Control (ASaC) platform. The platform is fitted with the new Searchwater 2000 AEW Cerberus system. 849 A Flight took the new Mk 7 Sea King to the front line in HMS *Ark Royal* in September 2002.

The key to the Cerberus system is a powerful pulse Doppler radar. This can identify targets over land and has multiple beams, enabling it to simultaneously track a large number of air and surface contacts, including aircraft or missiles at various heights. The radar also has an integrated IFF system. Information is displayed as an integrated picture on two screens without background clutter, as pulse doppler radar picks out only moving targets. The two displays are called Human Computer Interfaces, and are 20-inch flat colour screens combined with plasma touch, sensitive, interactive control panels operated by two observers. An INS/GPS Ring Laser Gyro Navigation system is fitted, plus a high-speed datalink to automatically transmit radar information to friendly ships and aircraft. For example, the tactical picture can be passed to the Sea Harrier pilot sitting on the deck ready to get airborne. These improvements should be 40% more effective, as well as being lighter and more reliable.

Number of observers on the Active Navy List: 323, of which 14 were under training, in 2002.

2002 – FAA OBSERVERS, Statistical Summary

Number of aircraft in which observers operated
Fixed Wing 27 (of which 13 were Jetstreams used for observer training and communications)
42 ASW Helicopters; 25 Sea Kings; 17 Merlin
50 Lynx Helicopters, ASW and Attack
10 AEW Sea King Helicopters

2003 – OBSERVER RECRUITMENT AND TRAINING

Initial training takes place at Britannia Royal Naval College, Dartmouth. Entry age for non-graduate officers is 17–26 and candidates must have at least five GCSEs Grade A–C and 140 UCAS (University Clearance Assessment Scheme) points.

These are awarded as follows:

A Level	Grade A = 120 points	A/S Level	Grade A = 60 points
	B = 100 points		B = 50 points
	C = 80 points		C = 40 points

TERM 1
Induction

During the first two weeks, days start very early and end very late, with the hours between filled with physical training, lectures, sport, parade training, boatwork, and sundry other tasks. Young officers quickly learn to organise their time, to prepare equipment and uniforms in advance, and fit more into a day than they would previously have thought possible.

Naval General Training

Training during Term 1 is designed to provide the professional knowledge and officer qualities, such as discipline, integrity, physical and moral courage, that are required in the Royal Navy today. The training includes practical boatwork, navigation, warfare, staff skills, engineering, meteorology and oceanography. Before embarking in their first warship for Initial Sea Training, in Term 2, all cadets complete a course of basic sea survival that includes fire-fighting, damage control and life-raft drills.

TERM 2
Initial Sea Training

For Term 2, cadets go to sea in a Type 22 Frigate. They live, and work, alongside junior ratings, the people young officers will soon find themselves leading. They will spend time in all the major departments on board, helping out with everything from preparing ship's company meals to taking part in warfare exercises. They will spend many hours watchkeeping on the bridge, shadowing engineering repair and maintenance, learning about pay and supply matters and watching or taking part in everything that a ship does at sea or alongside.

TERM 3
Aircrew

In this final term, all aircrew officers attend a course of science, engineering and strategic studies, biased towards aviation and the FAA, to support their subsequent aircrew training. Observers then undergo a three-week 'Grading' course at RNAS Culdrose. After two days in ground school, learning basic navigation and airmanship techniques, potential observers have two simulator trips and two flights in Jetstreams to prove they have the basic skills to make a good observer. Successful students then complete Term 3 with a three-week course of land and sea survival and aviation medicine.

Observer Training

The very intensive eight month Basic Observer Course (BOC) covers all aspects of air navigation, from the basics learnt on grading right through to the skills required of a front line observer flying in a RN helicopter. Basic tactics and aircraft captaincy are taught towards the end of the course. The observer must be able to fight the aircraft as well as navigate, and is expected to act as an airborne tactical commander. All flying (75 hours) is done in the Jetstream T2 and is backed up by training and instruction in the Radar Procedures Ground Trainer (RPGT) or simulator (56 hours).

On completion of the BOC, successful students will find out which squadron they will join for their Advanced Flying Training (AFT). With three options available, the student observer can look forward to joining either 702 NAS for Lynx training, 824 NAS for Merlin training, or 849 NAS for Sea King AEW training.

OPERATION TELIC – IRAQ, 2003

After Desert Storm, the ceasefire talks in March 1991 were followed by a UN resolution and agreement that Saddam Hussein should declare, and destroy, his chemical, biological and nuclear programmes and weapons. For 7 years the UN inspectors made slow progress in achieving verification of these objectives and, in 1998, the inspectors were expelled from Iraq. In November 2002 they were reluctantly readmitted, but little further evidence was produced to confirm the weapons had been destroyed. By January 2003 America and Britain agreed that military action was inevitable. The Task Force was in position at the beginning of March, and in the early hours of 20 March, Operation Telic commenced.

The main tasks of the British naval observers were to escort and protect the coalition warships and merchant ships to the theatre of operations, and to support the amphibious assault by the Royal Marines on the Al Faw peninsula.

Before and after Telic, the Lynx Mk 3 and Mk 8 helicopters of 815 NAS, operating from frigates and destroyers, had the main duty of force protection, particularly in areas which were likely danger spots for terrorist attack squads to operate; i.e. the Straits of Gibraltar, the Suez Canal, the entrance to the Red Sea and the Straits of Hormuz.

The deployment of the 3rd Cdo Brigade into the Al Faw peninsula was a crucial factor in the early stages of the war and was supported by 845 NAS, 849 NAS, and 18 Squadron RAF, operating from HMS *Ark Royal* and HMS *Ocean*. 845 NAS, flying Sea King Mk 4s, together with 18 Squadron flying Chinooks, carried troops and supplies in the largest helicopter-borne assault since the Vietnam War. Lynx and Gazelles of 847 NAS kept a watchful eye on the coastal waters and waterways of the Al Faw.

Operating from '*Ark*', 849 A Flight, in their Sea King Mk 7s, maintained a vital 24-hour overland airborne surveillance and control of aircraft striking in support of the Royal Marines. They also contributed to operations ashore by detecting land vehicles; providing detailed target information to naval and ground forces so they could successfully deal with enemy ground elements. Iraqi tanks and artillery were destroyed before they could threaten coalition troops. 814 NAS, in the first operational use of its Merlins, together with

820 NAS Sea King Mk 6s, operated a 24-hour surveillance of the whole of the north Arabian Gulf, providing protection against fast attack craft fitted with explosives. They also carried supplies from the RFAs *Fort Austin* and *Fort Victoria* to other task group units.

The combat phase of Telic lasted from 19 March to 9 April. Three weeks later, on 1 May, President Bush declared the major combat phase was over. During May '*Ark*' and '*Ocean*' returned to the UK.

At the time of writing, November 2003, many FAA helicopters are still detached with RN frigates, destroyers, and in RFAs supplying them. They are patrolling the Gulf to intercept hostile, or illegal, shipping.

The Observer is still in business!

BIBLIOGRAPHY

Fights and Flights – Charles Rumney Samson, 1930.
Republished Buttery Press Nashville, 1990

British Naval Aircraft Since 1912 – Owen Thetford, Putnam, 1962

Observers and Navigators – C G Jefford, Airlife, 2001

The Story of a North Sea Air Station – C F Snowden Gamble, OUP, 1928

The Fleet Air Arm History – Lt Cdr J Waterman RD RNR,
Old Bond Street Publishing Co., 1975

Seaplanes - Felixstowe – Gordon Kinsey, Dalton, 1978

Fly Navy – Fleet Air Arm Officers Association

Carrier Observer – Gordon Wallace, Airlife, 1978

Find Fix and Strike – John Winton, Batsford, 1980

Flight Deck - Falklands Edition – MOD, 1982

Wings at Sea – Gerard A Woods, Conway Maritime Press, 1985

Fly Navy View from the Cockpit 1945–2000 – Charles Manning,
Leo Cooper, 2000

Iraq Campaign 2003. Royal Navy and Royal Marines – Robert Fox,
Agenda Publishing, 2003

6

8

GLOSSARY

AB	Able Seaman	NAS	Naval Air Squadron
A/C	Aircraft	NF	Nightfighter
AEW	Airborne Early Warning	OPEC	Organisation of Petroleum Exporting Countries
AI	Airborne Interception Radar		
AFT	Advanced Flying Training	RFA	Royal Fleet Auxiliary
A/S	Anti-submarine	RNAS	Royal Naval Air Service
ASR	Air-sea Rescue	RNAS	Royal Naval Air Station
ASV	Air Surface Vessel	RNVR	Royal Naval Volunteer Reserve
ASW	Anti-submarine Warfare	R/P	Rocket Projectile
BRNC	Britannia Royal Naval College	Sonar	(airborne) – an active detection device, lowered into the sea from a helicopter. It transmits signals reflected off submerged submarines so as to reveal their position to the attacker
CCA	Carrier Controlled Approach		
Cdo	Commando		
CO	Commanding Officer		
FAW	All Weather Fighter		
FC	Flight Commander	Sono-buoys	Passive listening devices, dropped in a pattern on the last known position of a submarine. These buoys detect propeller noises and then transmit their bearings, so the submarine's position can be fixed and its course changes plotted
FG	Fighter Ground Attack		
FSL	Flight Sub Lieutenant		
GCA	Ground Controlled Approach		
GPS	Global Positioning System		
HAS	Anti-submarine Helicopter		
HASR	Air-sea Rescue Helicopter	TBR	Torpedo Bomber Reconnaissance
IFF	Identification Friend or Foe		
INS	Inertial Navigation System	TSR	Torpedo Strike Reconnaissance
ML	Mine Layer	W/T	Wireless Telegraph

68